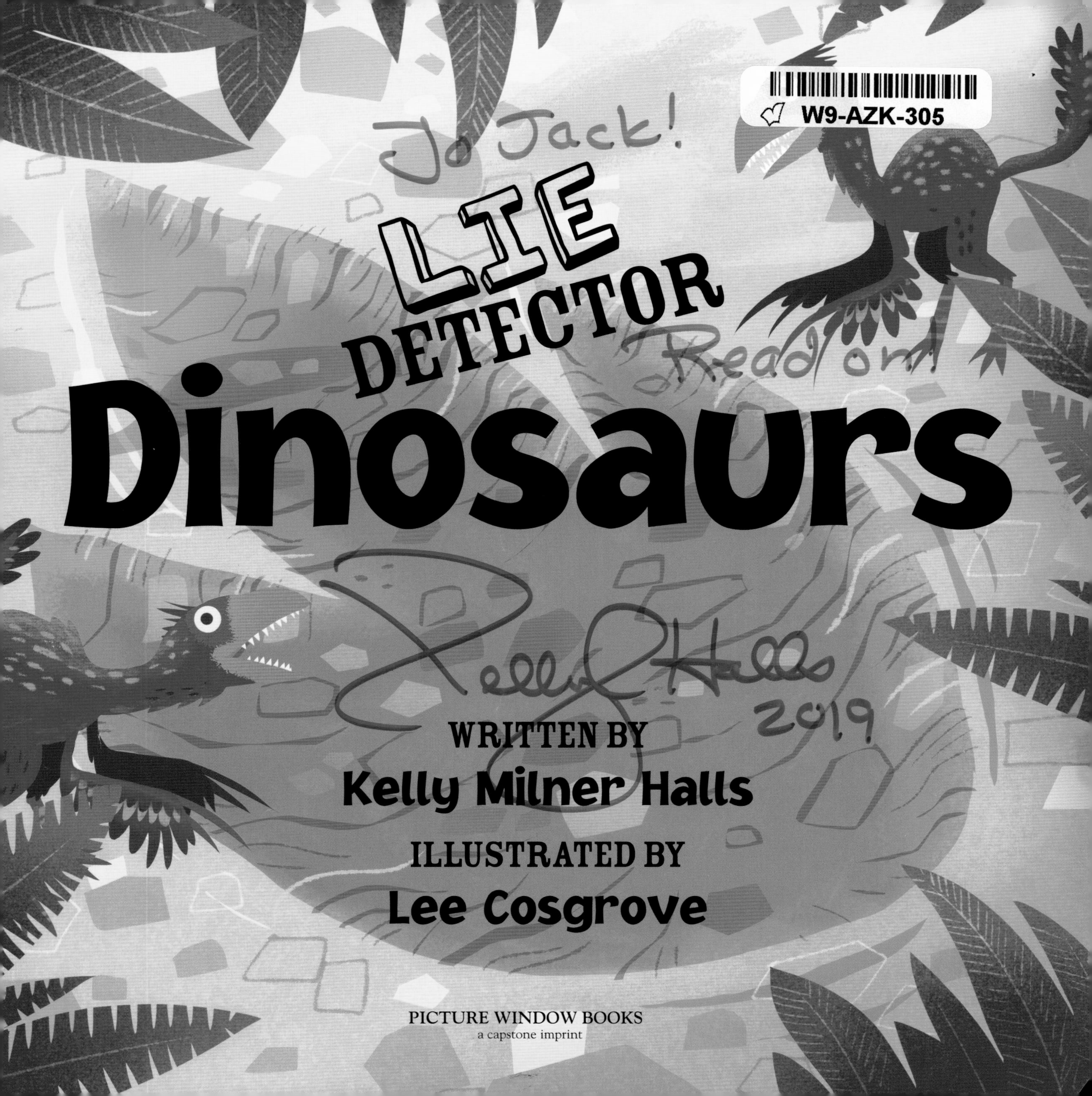

LIE DETECTOR

DETECTOR

Dinosaurs

WRITTEN BY

Kelly Milner Halls

ILLUSTRATED BY

Lee Cosgrove

PICTURE WINDOW BOOKS
a capstone imprint

Picture Window Books are published by
Capstone, 1710 Roe Crest Drive,
North Mankato, Minnesota 56003
www.capstonepub.com

© 2016 Weldon Owen
This edition by Picture Window Books,
a Capstone imprint.

Library of Congress
Cataloging-in-Publication Data
Cataloging-in-publication information is on file
with the Library of Congress.

ISBN 978-1-4795-8510-6 (hardcover)
ISBN 978-1-4795-8514-4 (paperback)
ISBN 978-1-4795-8518-2 (eBook PDF)

Written by Kelly Milner Halls

Printed in China
10 9 8 7 6 5 4 3 2 1

All photographs Shutterstock

LIE DETECTOR Dinosaurs

WRITTEN BY
Kelly Milner Halls

ILLUSTRATED BY
Lee Cosgrove

PICTURE WINDOW BOOKS
a capstone imprint

Can you find the secrets written in stone and prove you are the master of all things dinosaur?

Dinosaurs lived on Earth for more than 160 million years. Then they vanished. No one has ever seen a dinosaur, so how do we know they ever lived? The answer is simple. Dinosaurs left thousands of clues we call fossils. Fossils are remains of an animal or plant, preserved as rock.

Do you know the facts about fossils or the dirt on dinosaurs? Dig into these fun fact-or-fib questions to test your prehistoric knowledge.

FIB!

More than 700 kinds of dinosaurs have been unearthed. More are being found every day. Scientists think that many more are waiting to be discovered.

Super Sleuth

Kids have found new dinosaur species. An 8-year-old named Christopher Wolfe discovered the Zuniceratops in the United States.

FIB!

Epidendrosaurus was a dinosaur that could be as small as a sparrow. But Supersaurus was as long as three school buses lines up end-to-end!

ALL GROWN UP?

Many dino discoveries that were thought to be little adults turned out to be regular-sized babies. But some small dinosaurs were just small dinosaurs.

FIB!

Dinosaurs ruled over Earth during three different stretches of time known as periods. Brachiosaurus lived during the Jurassic Period. Triceratops, however, lived during a different period called the Cretaceous. The two dinosaurs never even had a chance to meet.

THE TRIASSIC PERIOD

THE JURASSIC PERIOD

THE CRETACEOUS PERIOD

FIB!

Dinosaur eggs came in many shapes and sizes—from the size of a golf ball to the size of a loaf of French bread. But they were not giant. So far, no dinosaur egg as big as a human has been discovered.

FACT!

Long-necked dinosaurs called sauropods swallowed stones on purpose. Those rocks helped to grind up the food inside their stomachs, even after they had finished chewing it with their teeth. Chickens do the same thing today.

All dinosaurs had **scaly** skin.

FACT or FIB?

15

FIB!

One of the smallest dinosaurs, Pegomastax from Africa, had porcupine-like quills. Many other dinosaurs had soft, downy feathers, especially when they first hatched.

FACT!

Many of the insects you see today also lived with your favorite dinosaurs. These insects include ants, bees, wasps, spiders, gnats, and mosquitoes.

FACT!

Archaeopteryx and Confuciusornis were feathered and could fly. Pterosaurs could fly too, but they were not dinosaurs. They were flying reptiles.

Whoa!

Yummy!

FIB!

Some carnivorous dinosaurs ate insects, including Mononykus! It used its long claws to dig out lots of ants from tree trunks and dirt hills!

TINY TERRORS

T. rex babies had weak legs when they first hatched. Their parents probably brought them meat to eat until they grew big enough to hunt for themselves.

Yuck!

FIB!

Tyrannosaurus rex had terrible breath! It ate meat, and some of its dinner got trapped between those giant dagger-like teeth. When the meat decayed, T. rex had terrible rotten breath.

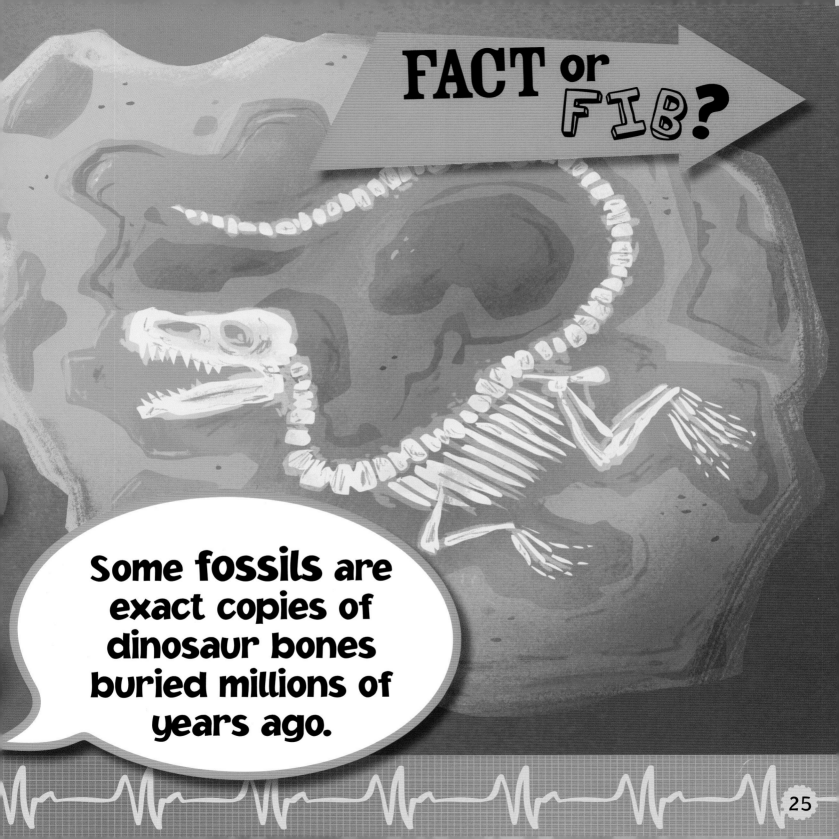

FACT or FIB?

Some **fossils** are exact copies of dinosaur bones buried millions of years ago.

Watch out! You know what happens if you get stuck in the tar pit!

FACT!

When a dinosaur bone is gently covered in dirt, minerals in the ground water seep into tiny holes in the bone. Little by little, the minerals fill the holes and harden into rock. As the bone disappears, minerals replace it, creating an exact copy. Different minerals create different-colored fossilized bones.

FACT!

Dinosaurs did become extinct 66 million years ago. Most dinosaur scientists believe that the main reason was a giant asteroid hitting Earth. When a 6-mile- (9.7-km-) wide space rock slams into a planet, it really means trouble. But other things like disease and volcanic gas may have made things even worse.

Super Sleuth

Asteroids can range from around the size of a pebble up to 621 miles (1000 km) across.

We need to evolve fast!

The end of an era ...

Losing the dinosaurs to extinction may seem a little sad. But who wants to be a midnight snack to a Tyrannosaurus rex? And even the nicest long-neck could still turn your house into firewood. Maybe fossilized dinosaurs are easier to love than the real thing. If not, follow the feathers! Dinosaur scientists think birds might be dinosaurs, cleverly evolved.

GUESS WHO!

No one knows for sure what dinosaurs looked like. They could have been brown, green, or even pink. Scientists know that some dinos had feathers, while others had scales. Dinosaur fossils also show that some of these prehistoric creatures had special horns, spiked tails, and a lot of other cool body parts. Take a look at each close-up and see if you can match it to the correct dinosaur name.

3. Who owns these bone-crunching teeth?

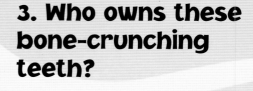

1. Which dinosaur had feathers like these?

2. Whose horns are these?

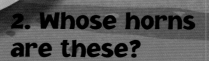

4. Which dinosaur had spiky quills instead of scales?

CHOOSE YOUR ANSWERS FROM THE NAMES BELOW:

A. Pegomastax

B. Triceratops

C. Tyrannosaurus rex

D. Mononykus

E. Archaeopteryx

5. Who used its long claws to eat insects?

GLOSSARY

asteroid—a rock (large or small) that travels round the Sun

carnivore—an animal that eats meat

evolve—to change very slowly over a long time

extinction—when a species dies out

fossil—the remains or traces of an animal or plant preserved as rock

mineral—a natural substance found in the ground. Most rocks are made up of more than one mineral

prehistoric—something that existed before humans began to record history

pterosaur—a flying reptile that lived at the same time as the dinosaurs

species—a group of living things. Two animals of the same species can have babies together

INDEX